W9-DBT-197

*The Wines and Wineries of
the Hudson River Valley*

The Wines and Wineries of the Hudson River Valley

BY ALAN R. MARTELL AND ALTON LONG

FOREWORD BY BARBARA ENSRUD

PHOTOGRAPHY BY LAURY A. EGAN

A NORFLEET PRESS BOOK

THE COUNTRYMAN PRESS
WOODSTOCK · VERMONT

A Norfleet Press Book
New York, New York

Published by The Countryman Press, Inc.
PO Box 175, Woodstock, Vermont 05091

FIRST EDITION

Text copyright © 1993 by Alan R. Martell and Alton Long
Photographs copyright © 1993 by Laury A. Egan
Foreword copyright © 1993 by Barbara Ensrud

All rights reserved.
No part of this book may be reproduced in any form or by any
electronic or mechanical means without permission in writing from
the publisher, except by reviewers who may quote brief passages.

Library of Congress Cataloguing-in-Publication Data

Alan R. Martell, 1939-
Alton Long, 1932-
The Wines and Wineries of the Hudson River Valley
1. Viticulture—New York State.   2. Wine and winemaking— New York State.
I. Egan, Laury A.   II. Title.
TP557.M35   1993
641.2'2'097473—dc20
92-34361
ISBN 0-88150-251-0

Editor: Carolyn L. Maxwell
Designer: Laury A. Egan
Producer: John G. Tucker
Composition: Princeton University Press
and Browne Book Composition, Inc.

1 2 3 4 5 6 7 8 9 10

Printed and bound in Hong Kong

Frontispiece: A window at Walker Valley Vineyards

Contents

Foreword

Traveling north from Manhattan, the train to Poughkeepsie rumbles along the Hudson River, reaching Croton Point in about an hour. I've taken it often, heading for the little river hamlet of Garrison where I've spent many a delightful weekend. At Croton Station, I used to gaze out on this picturesque protrusion of land, trying to visualize what it must have been like when there was a vineyard there instead of the park and playground that inhabit it today. What a site for a vineyard—overlooking the majestic Hudson with Bear Mountain looming across the water on the opposite shore and the bridge that leads to it silhouetted against the sky upriver.

New York boasts the country's oldest surviving wine industry and the focus of this book, the Hudson Valley, served as cradle for its first commercial vineyards. Indeed, as authors Alan Martell and Alton Long point out, the very seeds of American viticulture were sown here over 300 years ago—metaphorically speaking, of course: vines are generally propagated from cuttings rather than seeds. In 1677, French Huguenots planted vines near New Paltz, nearly a hundred years ahead of the first grapes planted in California. Some 150 years later, America's first commercial vineyard was established at Croton Point. Today, a thousand acres of vineyard dot the landscape either side of the river and the number of wineries has grown to 20.

As Hudson Valley wines are not as well known as those from other districts of New York, I am particularly delighted to welcome a book that puts a spotlight on a region that has steadily come into its own. I've watched the growth of Hudson Valley wineries with interest and admiration as they struggle against the odds.

Some of the biggest hurdles have been economic.

Finding a market that would accept the wines has long been a struggle. Having to overcome the poor image of New York wines as being "foxy" (or grapey) in flavor was undoubtedly harder than starting from scratch. The jelly-jar image of wines made from native grapes like Concord and Catawba was an albatross that New Yorkers couldn't shake until recently. Persistence has paid off, however; the old image is gradually fading as increasingly stylish wines appear in their stead.

Growers have also had to contend with the vagaries of weather, mostly temperate along the Hudson because of the broad deep river, but mercilessly treacherous on occasion, as in 1980. That was the year of the now-infamous Christmas massacre, a freeze so sudden and prolonged that it destroyed many vineyards and virtually wiped out existing stands of young vinifera. The growers persevered, however, and moved on; they pulled out the dead vines and planted new ones, hopeful, if not confident, that such catastrophe strikes only once in a hundred years.

There is still considerable controversy over the viability of growing vinifera in the Hudson Valley. Wineries like Millbrook and West Park relish the challenge; Rivendell, on the other hand, buys Chardonnay from the Finger Lakes and Chardonnay and Merlot from Long Island. (Interestingly, its most popular wine, Sarabande, comes mainly from locally grown Seyval Blanc.) I would remind the skeptical, however, that almost every region east of the Rockies was advised by the experts against growing vinifera—and almost everywhere the experts have been proved wrong. I am particularly pleased with the performance of Chardonnay here, produced in a style that evokes the appealing snap of crisp, fresh apples—perhaps not surprising in a region once devoted to some of the most distinctive and delectable apple varieties grown anywhere, among them Newtown Pippin, Cortland, and Northern Spy.

Until recently, the Hudson Valley has been something of a well-kept secret. A relatively small coterie of New Yorkers has long known the Hudson Valley to be a great getaway. The handsome Palisades on

From then on, some chose to stick to hardier species, largely the hybrids developed in France to withstand severe cold such as Seyval Blanc, Vidal, and Vignoles. Many of the older wineries have found their niche working solely with hybrids, such as Clinton Vineyards near Poughkeepsie, which produces still and sparkling Seyval. Cascade Mountain has made its mark with several well-crafted blends, particularly those making use of hybrid reds like Chancellor, Foch, and Leon Millot which admirably suit Hudson Valley foods and flavors. Within a couple of years after the disastrous freeze, a few intrepid vinifera growers appeared on the scene, willing to gamble on the region's potential—in spite of other threats from Mother Nature, such as late-spring frosts or rain during harvest.

the river's west bank and the rolling wooded hills east of it offer spectacular color in autumn. The countryside, with its orchards and vineyards and sleepy river villages, evokes a storybook landscape—a point best made, perhaps, by the owners of Rivendell, who named their winery after the magical place inhabited by Tolkien's hobbits. Photographer Laury Egan has captured much of its charm with her camera, but the vistas, the ambiance, and the tastes of the Hudson Valley are best experienced first-hand.

The revitalized wine industry of the Hudson Valley has made significant strides in the last decade, but in many respects it is still a work in progress. Some of the wines continue to show an awkwardness that betrays the amateur's lack of experience, but they are far fewer than they used to be. In years when it rains during harvest, the wines can be thin and lacking in flavor. But the number of balanced, flavorful wines is on the increase—and increasingly, notice is taken of them. Outside the region, there is greater acceptance of the wines than ever before, as recognition in national competition proves. Several New York restaurants feature Hudson Valley wines—by the bottle as well as by the glass. Many are available in New York City wine shops and more will be in the future. National media, including *The Wine Spectator* and *The New York Times*, have also documented their quality and progress.

This book, then, comes at a good juncture. In recent years, the number of tourists visiting the region has jumped dramatically and continues to grow. As Americans have grown more knowledgeable about wine and more relaxed about enjoying it, wineries have become a big draw. Rivendell, near New Paltz, claimed 40,000 visitors last year—a drop in the amphora, perhaps, compared with the million who visit Napa Valley's Robert Mondavi Winery annually, but nevertheless encouraging to the local vintners who sell most of their production right at the winery.

Based on their steady progress, Hudson Valley vintners and growers can feel good about their efforts and confident about the future. What I hope to see, as the vines develop more character and winemaking skills gain greater finesse, is an open-minded approach to blending. One of the significant trends in New World winemaking is a renewed respect for the art of blending. Varietally pure wines are no longer the only way to go, particularly in red wines, whether made from vinifera or hybrids. We are seeing it with white wines as well. Thoughtful experiment in this direction could yield some exciting wines in years to come. Meantime, there is much to enjoy while the quiet evolution continues to unfold.

BARBARA ENSRUD

Introduction

"Gathering Grapes in the Vineyard at Marlboro-on-the-Hudson," from *Frank Leslie's Illustrated Newspaper*, New York, October 18, 1879. (Courtesy of Benmarl Vineyards)

The Source

The Hudson River begins not with a roar or torrent, but with a trickle from tiny Lake Tear of the Clouds on Mount Marcy in the Adirondack Mountains. By the time it reaches New York Harbor and the Atlantic Ocean, some 315 miles downstream, it has become, by dint of hundreds of tributaries, one of the world's largest and most majestic rivers.

Its size enables ocean-going vessels to traverse nearly half its length from the Atlantic to Albany and smaller boats to Troy. In 1825, the completion of the Erie Canal connected the Hudson River to the Great Lakes and their waterways, opening America's "frontier" of upstate New York, the Midwest, and Canada to the exchange of large volumes of goods and produce.

The Hudson River Valley also has a rich and complex geology. Geologically defined as the Taconic Province, its soils are alternately comprised of shale, schist, slate, clay, gravelly loams, and limestone. The Palisades tower 550 feet above the Hudson's southern banks, while above Newburgh, the river cuts through the Shawangunk, Catskill, and Appalachian Mountains.

The river's water moderates the region's temperature and the valley's structure draws in maritime air from the Atlantic. These factors combine to create favorable growing conditions for a wide variety of grapes and other produce.

The valley's average annual precipitation is approximately 44 inches and its growing season ranges from 153 to 196 days. The Hudson Valley ranges in latitude from 41.5° to 43.5°, parallel with northern Spain, southern France, and central Italy. Though comparable to these areas in topography and vegetation, the Hudson Valley has more humidity and precipitation and is generally cooler.

Early History

The Hudson River Valley was first settled by the Algonquin Indians as early as 4000 B.C. Around 1300 A.D., they were joined by the Iroquois who formed a confederacy called The Five Nations in about 1570. The Florentine Giovanni da Verrazano and Portuguese Estavan Gomez are the first Europeans credited with sighting the river in 1524 and 1525. It was not fully navigated, however, until 1609, when Henry Hudson, an Englishman hired by the Dutch East India Company, explored the river aboard the *Half Moon* in search of a route to China. Records indicate the explorers' early encounters with native Americans resulted in trading for grapes, pumpkins, and animal skins.

Enthusiasm grew as word spread about the discovery of new land, and in 1623 the first band of Dutch arrived on their ship *New Netherlands* to establish settlements up and down the Atlantic coast. By 1626, a permanent foothold was established in New Amsterdam (later renamed New York by the English), and by 1640 the Hudson had become a major trading artery. By 1670, many German, English, Dutch, and Huguenot settlements thrived along its banks.

The Birth of an Industry

The Huguenots' purchase of New Paltz in 1677 marks the beginning of the Hudson Valley as a commercial grape-producing region, making it the oldest in the nation. Although literature about the period refers to local beer and the importation of rum and brandy, wine is seldom mentioned. This is understandable, as most families made wine in their own cellars. Leon Adams, a prominent writer on American wine, suggests that the Huguenots at New Paltz, like many European settlers, probably attempted to cultivate European grape varieties and, after failing, turned to native grapes for wine production.

There are no records which suggest the commercial distribution of locally made wines from the 1700s to the early 1800s. In view of the fact that New York City was a major port for imported goods, wines from Europe were readily available. Thus, it was probably grapes, not wine, which represented the primary Hudson Valley viticultural product sent to market.

The modern era of Hudson Valley grape—and eventually wine—production dates to the early 1800s. The story opens at Croton Point, a fertile piece of land jutting one-and-a-half miles into the Hudson River about 30 miles north of New York City (today part of the township of Croton-on-Hudson). Robert Underhill, a Quaker, purchased this land in 1804. Over the years, he established a self-sustaining community that produced watermelons, Newtown Pippin apples, pears, chestnuts, castor beans (from which castor oil is made), and bricks. In 1827, Underhill purchased some European vines, only to see them fail soon after planting.

Over the next two decades, Underhill's son Richard, with the help of a Rhineland vinedresser, began crossing native grapes with vinifera (European) varieties on 50 acres of land, yielding fruit with new and delicious flavors. Underhill's efforts soon inspired others. In 1845, William T. Cornell of Ulster County cultivated a vineyard of Isabella vines that intrigued his brother-in-law, Andrew Caywood. Originally from Modena, New York, Caywood settled in 1877 in Marlborough, where he remained until his death in 1889. He is credited with developing many second-generation hybrids that were quite successful—the most famous being the Dutchess grape, still grown today. Caywood's original vineyards are now part of Benmarl Vineyards and still tended by Mark Miller, the present owner.

By demonstrating that vinifera and native grape varieties could be successfully cross-bred, these pioneering vintners made an immense contribution to the region and, ultimately, to the Eastern wine industry.

In more recent times, two winemakers from New York's Finger Lakes region, the late Dr. Konstantin Frank and Hermann J. Wiemer, have also made lasting contributions to eastern wines, including those of the Hudson Valley. These men supplied—and Wiemer still does—Hudson Valley vintners with superior cuttings of European grape vines, particularly Chardonnay and Riesling.

The Early Wineries

The story of Jaques Brothers Winery, renamed Brotherhood in 1885, begins in 1837 when John

"Gathering Grapes—An October Scene on the Hudson," appeared in *Harper's*, October 26, 1867. Sketch depicts a vineyard near Newburgh, New York. At that time, some 25,000 acres in the valley were planted with grapes. (Courtesy of Benmarl Vineyards)

Jaques, a shoemaker and vintner, established a vineyard of Catawba and Isabella vines. Upon learning that these grapes would fetch a mere 13 cents per pound, Jaques decided to start a winery and began offering altar wines in 1839. Brotherhood, in Washingtonville, is our nation's oldest continuously operating winery.

The valley's second winery opened around 1850. Richard Underhill's successful grape-breeding efforts prompted him to build four subterranean brick caves on Croton Point (similar to, but smaller than Brotherhood's) to produce altar wines. From 1866 until 1873, Underhill marketed wine in New York City as a medicinal tonic. Although his vineyards no longer exist, the sturdy old caves remain in an area which is now a Westchester County park.

The region's third winery was also called Brotherhood at its inception, as it was owned by a utopian community named the Brotherhood of New Life. Founded by Thomas Harris Lake, a Universalist minister turned mystic, this socialist-religious community established its third home in Amenia, New York, in 1860. Wine, which Harris believed had divine and miraculous powers, became its main industry. The community remained in the area only until 1867, when it moved to Brocton, New York (and eventually to Fountain Grove, California, in 1875).

The Hudson Valley Wine Company in Highland,

John Jaques (1790-1876) established Jaques Brothers Winery in 1839. It was renamed Brotherhood in 1885. (Courtesy of E.J. McLaughlin)

A mid-19th-century poster from Jaques Brothers Winery. The original buildings and vineyards remain the core of Brotherhood's operations. (Courtesy of E.J. McLaughlin)

built by Alphonso Bolognesi in 1904 as a summer estate, was the region's fourth winery. During its formative years, the estate used Delaware and Catawba grapes to make altar wines for local monasteries. Now called Regent Champagne Cellars, it is still in operation.

Not surprisingly, Prohibition, from 1919 to 1933, had little effect on the region's wine industry. Table grapes were the primary vineyard crop and there were only two wineries in operation, both making government-approved altar wines.

Marlborough Champagne Cellars was the first winery established after Prohibition. Founded in 1944 by Arnold Kneitel, Marlborough initially produced kosher sparkling wines from native American and local hybrid grapes and was a major supplier of New York City's banquet halls. In 1976, it was renamed the Great River Winery, then renamed again when purchased in 1980 by Windsor Vineyards of California. A tasting and sales room are maintained in the original historic building in Marlborough, which sells wines made from California grapes.

Near New York City in Rockland County lies now-closed High Tor Vineyards, once one of the East's most prominent small wineries. Made famous by Maxwell Anderson's play *High Tor*, this craggy mountain site was purchased in 1949 by the prominent journalist Everett Crosby as fulfillment of a dream born while caring for a grapevine from his Manhattan rooftop garden. High Tor wines were made from hybrid grapes and placed on the wine lists of many of New York City's finest restaurants.

Crosby made a valiant but unsuccessful attempt to change a New York State law which then required

wineries to pay a $1,000 annual licensing fee. He argued, with moral support from fellow wine lovers and professionals, that this fee made it difficult for winemakers at small operations to earn a living. Crosby wrote a moving and often humorous account of his years at High Tor in his book, *The Vintage Years*.

The Landmark Farm Winery Act

During the early 1970s, New York's large commercial wineries dramatically cut back on the amount of local grapes they purchased, replacing them with juice brought by truck from California. As grape growers in the Finger Lakes lost their market, a few paid the exorbitant fees and opened as wineries. The turning point came in 1975, when a grape glut threatened to topple the Finger Lakes grape industry. Pressure mounted for loosening the grip of the State's archaic, temperance-based laws. Hugh Carey, the newly elected Governor, was sympathetic and named John S. Dyson Commissioner of Agriculture. Dyson, a wine enthusiast, recognized the value of a healthy wine

1860s wine labels from Jaques Brothers Winery. (Courtesy of E.J. McLaughlin)

industry based on locally grown fruit. A task force was named and a Farm Winery Bill was drawn up.

Based on testimony by Benmarl's Mark Miller, the support of such prominent wine writers as Frank Prial, and the efforts of scores of local wine lovers and winemakers, New York's Farm Winery Act was signed into law on June 4, 1976. Miller's winery was given Farm Winery License Number One for his efforts and November was proclaimed "New York State Wine Month," culminating in an unprecedented tasting of New York wines at Manhattan's Four Seasons restaurant. After 43 years, with license fees now reduced to $125, it once again became feasible to earn a living from a small farm winery.

A Viticultural Name is Chosen

In 1978, the Bureau of Alcohol, Tobacco and Firearms (BATF) changed regulations as to how American wine regions could identify themselves. Before then, the valley's wine labels usually indicated that the wine had been made in the "Hudson River Valley" and most local winemakers preferred this term (even though a few of the wineries were outside the Hudson Valley proper). However, because Regent Champagne Cellars was then called "The Hudson Valley Wine Company," BATF disallowed the term as being too similar and, on July 6, 1982, "Hudson River Region" became an official appellation.

The region encompasses some 3,500 square miles and includes 1.6 million acres of land, with almost 1,000 acres planted in grapes. Ninety percent of the vineyard land is located in Columbia and Ulster counties.

Hudson Valley Wines in Perspective

From 1677 to 1975, a mere eight wineries opened in the Hudson Valley. The Farm Winery Act in 1976 provided the impetus for 24 new wineries to open their doors. In the last decade, a handful of these have closed: High Tor, Northeast, Cagnasso, Cottage, Eaton, and Woodstock.

At present, there are 23 wineries operating in the valley. This book features the 20 which use primarily New York State produce and are open to the public for tasting and tours. Not covered are Ashkol in Middletown, producer of kosher wines and grape juice; Windsor Vineyards in Marlborough, now a shop for the company's California wines; and the Riverview Tasting Room, also in Marlborough, which is currently formulating future plans. In addition,

On June 4, 1976, New York State Governor Hugh Carey signed the Farm Winery Act into law, enabling scores of new wineries to open. At his left is Mark Miller of Benmarl Vineyards, the new law's principal advocate. Behind the Governor are Assemblyman Dan Walsh, Commissioner Roger Barber, and Senator Richard Schermerhorn.

Union Vale Vineyards in Union Vale (east of Poughkeepsie) is scheduled to open as a winery in 1994.

The Hudson Valley is one of four viticultural regions that comprise New York State's wine industry, the country's largest outside of California. The three other regions are the Finger Lakes, Eastern Long Island, and Lake Erie. Collectively, these regions support some 95 bonded wineries.

The future of winemaking in the Hudson Valley looks bright. This is partly because the valley has always offered the visitor much in addition to wine. The region has compelling natural beauty and some of the most historic places and structures in all of New World America.

Perhaps most important to the valley's wineries is a shift taking place with much of the American public. Increasingly, we are awakening to the joy, and value, of buying fine local produce from our own communities. A bottle of local wine is a magnificent example of such produce—it celebrates the bounty of our own soil.

ALAN R. MARTELL

ALTON LONG

1 Walker Valley
 Vineyards

2 Brotherhood Winery

3 Brimstone Hill
 Vineyard

4 Baldwin Vineyards

5 Magnanini Winery

6 Adair Vineyards

7 Rivendell Winery

8 Benmarl Vineyards

9 Royal Kedem Winery

10 Regent Champagne
 Cellars

11 West Park Wine Cellars

12 El Paso Winery

13 Larry's Vineyard

14 Johnston's Winery

15 North Salem Vineyards

16 Amberleaf Vineyards

17 Millbrook Vineyards

18 Clinton Vineyards

19 Cascade Mountain
 Winery

20 The Meadery at
 Greenwich

Scale: One inch = 10 miles

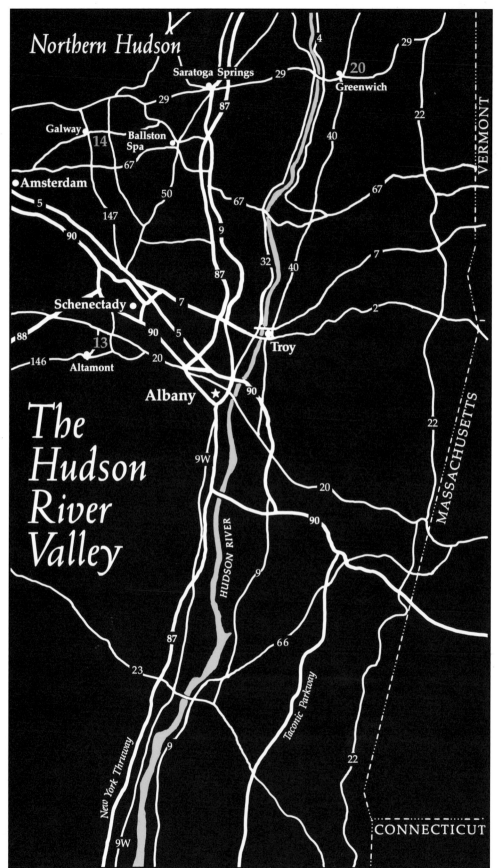

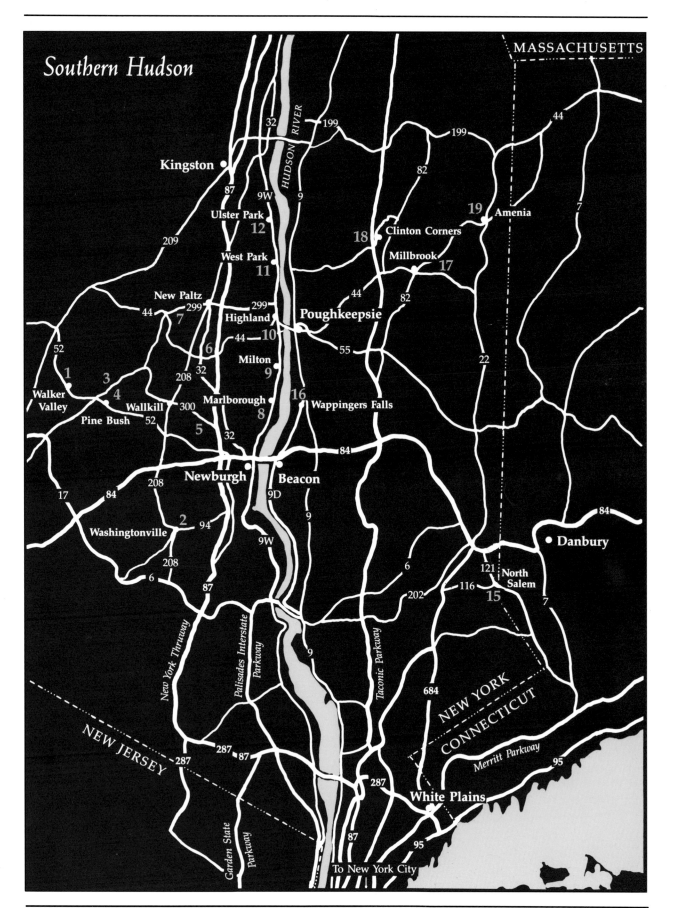

Southern Hudson

MASSACHUSETTS

HUDSON RIVER

Kingston

32

199

199

44

87

9W

9

82

Ulster Park

12

19 Amenia

18 Clinton Corners

West Park

11

Millbrook

17

New Paltz

209

44

299

299

44

7

Highland

10

Poughkeepsie

52

6

44

82

1

32

Milton

55

22

3

208

9

4

Walker
Valley

300

Marlborough

16

Wallkill

8

Wappingers Falls

Pine Bush

52

5

32

84

208

Newburgh

Beacon

9D

17

84

2

94

9

Washingtonville

9W

Danbury

84

208

6

202

121

North
Salem

6

87

116

15

7

New York Thruway

Palisades Interstate Parkway

Taconic Parkway

684

NEW YORK

CONNECTICUT

Garden State Parkway

NEW JERSEY

287

287

87

Merritt Parkway

95

287

White Plains

87

95

To New York City

~ 15 ~

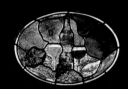

West of the River

Wine is constant proof that God loves us
and loves to see us happy.

BENJAMIN FRANKLIN
1706-1790
American Author,
Scientist and Diplomat

✓‿✓ *Walker Valley Vineyards* ‿✓

ESTABLISHED 1978

WALKER VALLEY

Gently sloping hills and fieldstone walls make Walker Valley Vineyards a picturesque place to visit. What brought founder and winemaker Gary Dross to this 106-acre site in 1970 was its fertile soil and natural drainage. In 1974 Dross planted his first vines, intending simply to sell the grapes at market. "Within a year or two," he says, "it occurred to me that making wine might be more fulfilling and possibly more profitable than growing grapes. I began speaking with industry professionals, I enrolled in workshops and conferences, and in general learned all I could about winemaking." In 1978, the year he obtained his license, Dross made 350 gallons of wine. He currently produces about 5,000 gallons annually and aims to expand to about 7,000.

Dross speaks optimistically about the future of wine in the Hudson Valley and his role in it. "My operating philosophy is that people have a good sense for wine and know what they like. I prefer dry wines. But, by letting the public educate me as to what they like and why, I soon began to make a wide range of wines from dry to semi-sweet." Dross responded to the demand for European varietals by planting Chardonnay vines.

Walker Valley also offers a selection of hybrids and fruit wines, including well-made Seyval Blanc, Ravat, Vidal, and a complex, oak-aged Foch. Dross's proprietary Serendipity, a blend of 75% Cayuga grapes and 25% strawberries, is a tasty sipping wine. Dross has also recently planted apple orchards bearing some 10 varieties for blending into apple wines.

West Point Academy, some 40 miles southeast of Walker Valley, has honored Dross the past five years by pouring his wines for its graduation banquets. Each year, Dross updates his labels with a reproduction of the graduating class's crest.

State Route 52, Walker Valley, NY 12588; 914-744-3449. Open daily, late spring through October; open weekends all year. Located on Route 52, 4 miles west of Pine Bush.

Brotherhood Winery

ESTABLISHED 1839

WASHINGTONVILLE

Founded in 1839, Brotherhood is America's oldest continuously operated .winery. By producing government-sanctioned altar and medicinal wines, Brotherhood was able to stay in business during Prohibition. As winemaker Cesar Baeza proudly declares, "Since our founding more than 150 years ago, Brotherhood has never missed a harvest."

Brotherhood's most historic structure is the John Jaques Building, constructed in 1823 and named after the winery's founder. This building, which today contains a café and art and antiques gallery, also provides access to the winery's impressive network of old subterranean caves. It is here, within the naturally cool climate maintained by thick brick walls, that wines are aged in all sorts of oak vessels—from massive casks dating from the 1840s to smaller, fresh-wood barrels imported from France. Baeza adds, "The original old casks still play an important role here—they age our fortified wines, our ports and sherries."

Jaques's sons operated the winery after his death in 1868. Since then, it has changed hands only three times; most recently in 1987, when purchased by a group of partners. Among them was Cesar Baeza, a native of Chile with winemaking experience in France and California. Baeza reflects on his choice to work in the Hudson Valley: "I realized that coming to Brotherhood represented an opportunity to produce fine wine at a place where history and tradition are unmatched."

Today, Brotherhood produces an extensive array of wines, including basic table wines like Chablis, Blush Chablis, and Burgundy; fortified wines; dessert wines; and premium varietal wines from Chardonnay, Riesling, Cabernet Sauvignon, and Pinot Noir.

35 North Street, Washingtonville, NY 10992; 914-496-3661. Open daily. From Route 208 north in Washingtonville, turn right on Main Street, then left to Brotherhood Plaza Drive.

Brimstone Hill Vineyard

ESTABLISHED 1979

PINE BUSH

There is nothing quite like planting and caring for a row of vines, harvesting and pressing the grape bounty, then making and bottling a finished wine. It is humbling and there is a part of the winemaker's soul in each bottle. Operating Brimstone Hill Vineyard provides this opportunity for owners Richard and Valerie Eldridge.

Valerie, whose parents owned a winery in Anjou, France, grew up with a realistic appreciation of the labor required to run a winery. Richard, on the other hand, became enamored with the romance of wine soon after visiting his in-laws' operation. In 1966, Richard started making wine as an amateur. Two years later, he and Valerie bought their current property, and a year after that, planted their first grapes. After honing their skills, they opened their winery in 1979.

Brimstone Hill wines are made from hybrids and European varietals and range from a dry méthode champenoise sparkling wine of Seyval and Vidal to soundly made country wine blends. All but one are dry. Brimstone Hill's Seyval Blanc was served to President Reagan at a state dinner in 1986.

Richard says, "Our goal is simple: to interact personally with each customer and sell all our wine at the winery. This allows us to stay small and concentrate on what we do best—making quality wines—without having to deal with marketing. Competing in stores would be a whole different world."

Brimstone Hill Road 49, Pine Bush, NY 12566; 914-744-2231. Open daily in summer, except for Tuesdays and Wednesdays; open weekends all year. Take Route 52 west from Pine Bush to 7 north. Brimstone Hill Road is ½ mile on left.

Baldwin Vineyards

ESTABLISHED 1982

PINE BUSH

Wine was not an important part of early family life for either Jack or Patricia Baldwin, owners of Baldwin Vineyards. Then, in 1974, they traveled to France and discovered the joy of wine. Upon returning, they learned all they could about wine and winemaking. Jack reflects, "I worked as a marketing executive for a large pharmaceutical company, a job far removed from the art and science of winemaking. I had no interest in agriculture. I didn't have a garden and even disliked mowing the lawn."

Patricia convinced Jack that winemaking might be a desirable way to earn a living. In 1982, they founded their winery on a vineyard site dating from 1786. They learned from scratch and improvised as they went along: "We rented a tractor and I worked in dress shoes, the only shoes I had," Baldwin remembers. "That first year, we hoed by hand and planted some five acres of vines. We purchased juice from vineyards in the Finger Lakes. Fortunately for us, the wine industry is filled with people who love to help others get started." To Baldwin's amazement, he has met the challenges of agriculture and loves his work. They now have first-rate equipment and purchase only 15% of their grapes to produce 5,000 gallons of wine, most of which is sold at the winery.

The Baldwins produce ten wines which are mostly dry or off-dry, aged in stainless or oak, fruity or austere, according to the French or Germanic style desired. They specialize in Chardonnay and Cabernet Sauvignon, but their Claret (oak-aged 100% Chancellor) and Landot Noir are equally impressive. In the Baldwins' third year, *The Wine Spectator* awarded their Landot Noir a 96, an exceptionally high rating.

Hardenburgh Estate, Pine Bush, NY 12566; 914-744-2226. Open daily in summer, long weekends in spring and fall, and weekends in winter. Take Maple Avenue north from Route 52 in Pine Bush, then turn left on Hardenburgh Road. The winery is ⅕ mile on the right.

Magnanini Winery

ESTABLISHED 1983

WALLKILL

If you have the good fortune of arriving at Magnanini Winery for Saturday supper or Sunday lunch, you might believe you've stepped into an Italian cantina. Here, the aromas of warm food, tables laden with wine and fruit, and dancing to live accordion music combine, as Galba Magnanini explains, "to recreate our family's northern Italian heritage here in America."

Galba, Italy's 1948 ski-jumping champion, and his two brothers arrived in the United States in 1953 and established a construction and marble business in the Hudson Valley. In 1970, when Galba's son, Richard, expressed interest in growing grapes and making wine, the father was thrilled. They obtained advice and vines from cousin Donald Ziraldo, co-founder of Inniskillin, one of Canada's most prominent wineries, and viticultural recommendations from Cornell. Soon after, their vineyard was born.

The Magnaninis sold their grapes to Brotherhood until 1983, when they opened their winery and restaurant. Today, they produce six country wines—a Seyval Blanc and De-Chaunac, as well as four hybrid blends, ranging from dry to sweet.

172 Strawridge Road, Wallkill, NY 12589; 914-895-2767. Open daily, April to December. Reservations for restaurant. From Wallkill, take Route 300 east one mile, turn right on Plains Road, then turn right on Strawridge Road.

Adair Vineyards

ESTABLISHED 1987

NEW PALTZ

While it was the favorable soil and climate that brought Jim and Gloria Adair to this part of the valley to establish a vineyard, it was the beauty of the landscape and character of the buildings that prompted them to select this particular site, a 200-year-old farm. The winery itself occupies the property's handsome old barn, designated a National Historic Landmark in 1978. A plaque at its entrance reads "Thaddeus Hait—Farm, National Register, c. 1800."

Originally from Michigan, the Adairs developed a love of wine while living in an old Italian section of Brooklyn. "Winemaking was standard practice in our neighborhood," Jim Adair says. "Virtually every brownstone had a winepress bolted to the cellar floor." As their interest grew, the Adairs decided to plant a hobby vineyard of 100 vines in rural Washington County east of the Hudson. Adair smiles, "We learned quickly to appreciate the joys, and the challenges, of growing our own grapes."

Today, most Adair wines are made from locally grown grapes. They have eleven acres planted in Seyval Blanc, Foch, Ravat, and Leon Millot. They also produce Chardonnay and Baco Noir from grapes grown in the Finger Lakes region.

The Adair label design incorporates *The Solitary Oak*, a mid-19th-century painting by Asher B. Durand, a leader of the Hudson River School. The painting depicts a beautiful oak tree in a pastoral setting similar to the magnificent tree at the vineyard's entrance. But the story continues! On a recent trip to Ireland, Jim visited the village of Adare, where he sought to learn the relationship between its name and his own. His research revealed that "Adair" was a frequently used variation of "Adare" and led him to meet Lady Adare, who enlightened him on the meaning of their commonly held name. In old Gaelic, Adair means "oak by the ford."

75 Allhusen Road, New Paltz, NY 12561; 914-255-1377. Open daily. The winery is 6 miles south of New Paltz. From Route 32, turn east on Allhusen Road.

Rivendell Winery

ESTABLISHED 1983

NEW PALTZ

Rivendell has a wide selection of European and hybrid varietals that collectively have won more than 100 medals since 1989. Many of the hybrids bear proprietary names: Sarabande (named for a Spanish dance); Tear of the Clouds (named for the Hudson River's lake source); Interlude, a blush wine; Northern Lights, a light, spritzy wine; and Après, a dessert wine.

714 Albany Post Road, New Paltz, NY 12561; 914-255-0892. Open daily. Take Route 299 west from New Paltz, then turn left on Libertyville Road and follow signs to winery.

Six years ago, Jack Ransom and his three sons took a hard look at the security business they were operating and concluded two things: they were not having fun and they were not making the sort of contribution they would like. Rivendell is the result of their search for a business that supported their creative and entrepreneurial aspirations.

In 1987, the Ransoms purchased the 55-acre winery and vineyard. "When we bought this property," Ransom recalls, "we declared a mission that has not changed: to be a prominent and profitable winery, recognized for hand-crafted, quality wines."

They're off to an impressive start. With production of 35,000 gallons a year, Rivendell is already one of the valley's larger wineries. The Ransoms aim to eventually reach 100,000 gallons.

The Ransoms currently purchase 85% of their grapes from New York vineyards, a practice which reflects a specific blending philosophy. For example, they purchase Chardonnay grapes from vineyards throughout New York, prepare and oak-age each source separately, and then blend them to create three distinct Chardonnays.

The winery's name is taken from the mythological place in J.R.R. Tolkien's classic fairytale, *The Hobbit,* where Rivendell is "a refuge for all folks of goodwill."

Benmarl Vineyards

Sitting high on a hill overlooking the Hudson, Benmarl Vineyards—named in Gaelic for its slatey soil—is one of the country's oldest. Back in 1867, pioneering viticulturalist Andrew Caywood developed the Dutchess grape on this site.

Mark Miller, Benmarl's owner and founder, purchased this land and its original vines in 1956, intending to establish a hobby vineyard. The result, however, has become a lasting contribution to the Eastern wine industry. The passage of New York's Farm Winery Act in 1976 was due largely to Miller's efforts.

Today, Miller is a highly regarded American winemaker. At an assembly of wine-industry professionals at the United Nations in 1985, the renowned French oenologist Emile Peynaud saluted Miller as one of the world's 20 best winemakers. Only two other Americans, Californians Robert Mondavi and Richard Peterson, were included on Peynaud's list.

Miller is also an artist and author. The winery has an art gallery that displays his paintings and sells prints. And his book, *Wine: A Gentleman's Game*, chronicles his career as an illustrator, through his years in the Burgundy region of France, to his life as a winemaker.

While in France, Miller was elected to the celebrated Burgundian wine society, La Confrérie des Chevaliers du Tastevin. "The invitation to join the society," Miller says, "had more to do with my being an American and an artist than a wine connoisseur. I was regarded as something of a novelty. It is also true that my passion for wine was born during those years."

Miller's experience in Burgundy continues to influence his winemaking technique. Most of his red wines and even a few of his whites are aged extensively in small French-oak bar-

rels. Benmarl produces an Estate Red and an Estate White, both dry, several specialty wines, and a sparkling Verdelet and Seyval Blanc blend using the méthode champenoise. One of Benmarl's unique features is its Société des Vignerons, a program in which members support the vineyard by helping with the harvest and purchasing wines. Benmarl produces 10,000 cases each year, most of which goes to Société members.

Winemaking has become a family tradition. Miller's son Eric, winemaker at Benmarl from 1973 to 1979, is the co-owner and award-winning winemaker of the Chaddsford Winery in Pennsylvania.

Box 549, Highland Avenue, Marlborough, NY 12542; 914-236-4265. Winery open daily; The Bistro open Friday through Sunday. Take Western Avenue west from 9W in Marlborough, then turn left on Highland Avenue. Travel ½ mile to sign.

Royal Kedem Winery

ESTABLISHED 1949

MARLBOROUGH-ON-HUDSON

Few American wineries can match the family history of Royal Kedem. In 1848, the Herzog family was sole supplier of wine to Emperor Franz Josef I of Austria. Since then, eight generations of Herzogs have kept family tradition alive. Fleeing the tyranny of Eastern Europe in 1948, with $3,000 and his wine formulas safely recorded, Eugene Herzog first worked for the Royal Wine Corporation. By 1958, he and his son Ernest bought the company, adding the name Kedem (Yiddish for "forward" or "renew our days as before"). Upon Ernest's death in 1989, his son Michael took over as manager and winemaker.

Royal Kedem has facilities in Marlborough, Milton, and Brooklyn. The grapes are grown in Marlborough, where the wine is produced in a modern, high-tech facility that includes a tasting room. Visitors to the Milton operation follow a cobblestone path to a tasting room and shop which occupy a 130-year-old train station overlooking the river.

Royal Kedem uses New York-grown grapes and produces 1.5 million gallons of juice, half of which is made into wine before being sent to the Brooklyn facility for bottling. The family-run corporation now includes the Herzog Winery in California and an extensive line of imported kosher wines.

Over 25 kosher wines, made from local hybrid and native American grapes and in styles ranging from dry to sweet, can be found at the Marlborough tasting room. (Although the most common kosher wines are sweet, neither process nor tradition dictates they be so.) "I am encouraged to see more and more consumers appreciating good local wines made from healthy native and hybrid grapes," Michael affirms.

1519 Route 9W, Marlborough, NY 12542; 914-236-4281. Open Fridays and Sundays. Located 1¼ miles north of Marlborough on Route 9W.

Dock Road, Milton, NY 12547; 914-795-2240. Open daily except Saturdays. Located 3 miles north of Marlborough and just south of Milton on 9W.

Regent Champagne Cellars

Regent Champagne Cellars occupies an important place in the history of America and the Hudson Valley wine industry. The property's original vineyards, now old and overgrown, frame a picturesque view along Blue Point Road which leads to the winery's complex—stone buildings, courtyard, clocktower, and house replicating the layout of an Italian manor. Blue Point itself is a rocky overlook used by the Colonial Army during the Revolutionary War as its second line of defense after West Point. The winery's buildings are situated atop this steep bluff and command beautiful vistas of the river and valley.

Regent is the valley's second oldest winery. In 1904, Alphonso (Alexander) Bolognesi, a New York City investment banker, bought 325 acres along the Hudson and built a private summer estate. After the 1929 crash, he settled into the property, planting vineyards and establishing a winery that made still and sparkling wines. The estate operated as a self-sustaining business called the Hudson Valley Wine Company. In 1969, it was bought by Monsieur Henri Wines and opened to the public; Herbert Feinberg, the present owner, purchased it a few years later.

The winery was renamed Regent Champagne Cellars in 1987 when Ed Gogel, a wine industry veteran with forty years' experience, became its vice president. Gogel believes that native and hybrid grapes are better suited to this area than the more delicate European varieties. "That's why all of our wines have been made from the same local grapes, Delaware and Catawba, for more than eighty years. They've proved their mettle," he says.

Regent produces 4,000 gallons of sparkling wine annually and is reviving its long tradition of producing New York State "Champagne." Cur-

rently available are six charmat-produced sparkling wines: Brut Champagne and fruit-flavored Blueberry, Raspberry, Peach, Almond, and Strawberry. The winery is available for private parties and tours of 20 or more people.

200 Blue Point Road, Highland, NY 12528; 914-691-7296. Open weekdays; groups may arrange weekend visits. Closed mid-December to spring. From Route 9W about two miles south of Highland, turn east on Blue Point Road.

West Park Wine Cellars

ESTABLISHED 1983

WEST PARK

A 160-year-old barn is the centerpiece and ten acres of trellised grapevines are the backdrop for West Park Wine Cellars. Beyond a place to transform grapes into wine, it is also an environment, explains owner Lou Fiore, where "people come to eat good food, drink good wine, and enjoy each other's company."

As a trustee of local Iona College (operated by the Christian Brothers Order from Ireland), Fiore became fascinated with a dairy farm owned by the Order that had become virtually idle. All agreed the property was worth saving as a productive piece of land. So the farm, cleared of rocks and its soil tested by Cornell's agricultural labs, was sold to Fiore and converted into vineyards and a winery with ample room for indoor and outdoor gatherings.

Within the envelope of the old fieldstone barn, Fiore has built a modern winery. The animal stalls have been replaced by barrels, tanks, and equipment, and a state-of-the-art kitchen has been installed for catering. Fiore depends on students and faculty from the Culinary Institute of America, across the river in Hyde Park, to staff his needs at the winery. Dinner parties are integral to West Park's program and feature candlelit tables, classical music, and multi-course gourmet meals.

Fiore makes one wine, Chardonnay, in one style, French. Fiore credits wine expert Kevin Zraly with the decision to produce one European varietal. "Kevin's recommendation," Fiore adds, "was also in tune with my philosophy that it's better to do one thing well than many things less than well."

Fiore believes firmly in the value of education. Before opening the winery in 1983, he studied at Geisenheim in Germany, at the University of California at Davis, and under Hermann J. Wiemer in the Finger Lakes, who taught him grafting and planting techniques.

Fiore aims to increase production from 2,500 to 4,000 gallons annually, but will do so only if able to raise the quality of his wine to new plateaus each year. For example, he chose not to sell any of his 1990 vintage because it did not meet his standards.

9W & Burroughs Drive, Box 280, West Park, NY 12493; 914-384-6709. Open weekends, March until December. The winery is on 9W, just south of West Park.

El Paso Winery

ESTABLISHED 1981

ULSTER PARK

Felipe Beltra, owner of El Paso Winery, grew up in Uruguay and worked at his father's winery, which produced as much as 100,000 gallons annually. At age 16, he inherited responsibility for the operation. Nine years later, the business fell on hard times and Beltra decided to emigrate to the United States.

He arrived in New York in 1968. It would be eight years before New York State's Farm Winery law would be passed. In the meantime, Beltra's dreams of operating a winery began to fade. Then, in 1977, Ernest Herzog, head of Royal Wine Corporation, brought his dream back into focus. Sitting idle on the company's land along Route 9W was a tiny 150-year-old barn. Beltra gratefully recalls how Herzog not only helped him obtain the property, but also gave him business and viticultural advice. "Without Ernest Herzog," Beltra states, "there would be no El Paso Winery."

In stark contrast to his family's winery, Beltra makes and sells all 3,000 gallons of his wines by Christmas each year. He then returns to his homeland to spend time with his family.

The wines of El Paso are clean country wines made from a variety of grapes, including Seyval Blanc and Concord. They range from dry to sweet.

742 Broadway (Route 9W), Ulster Park, NY 12487; 914-331-8642. Open daily; closed January through March. The winery is on 9W, 4 miles south of Kingston.

~ Larry's Vineyard ~

ESTABLISHED 1989

ALTAMONT

Near the northern end of the Hudson Valley, Larry Grossi defies the colder climate by producing an impressive group of estate-bottled New York wines.

Grossi selected a site on a south-facing slope in an area southwest of Albany known for fine apple orchards. He attributes his success to healthy, single-trunk vines able to withstand cold winter temperatures.

Grossi has 15 acres under cultivation. In addition to several well-known hybrid grapes—Cayuga, Seyval Blanc, DeChaunac, and Foch—Grossi has many unusual varieties. These include King of the North, which grows wild in Montana; Reliance, developed by the University of Arkansas; and Edelweiss, Ventura, and Swenson from Minnesota. Grossi has also planted an experimental

vineyard with Melody, Ravat, and several Italian varieties.

Grossi makes wine with an all-natural approach. "I don't put chemicals on my grapes and I don't add sugar to my wine," he affirms. "In fact, if necessary, I won't pick my grapes until December to get the right sugar content." Grossi is also experimenting with technique. He ages his Edelweiss in a chestnut barrel and plans to test the "governo" process, used in his native Tuscany, in which the juice from small bunches of dried grapes is used to impart richness.

Grossi's friends and customers have noted that "Larry's Vineyard" does not sound as serious as his wines; they have encouraged him to try a new name, "Grossi Hill Winery." "But," says Grossi, "it would still be the same wine."

R.D. 1, Box 284B, Furbeck Road, Altamont, NY 12009; 518-355-7365. Open from spring until December; closed Mondays and Tuesdays. Travel on Route 20 west from Albany to intersection with 158. Continue on 20 for 3 miles, then turn left on Settle Hill Road. Follow signs to winery.

Johnston's Winery

ESTABLISHED 1991

GALWAY

Located in an old barn at the foothills of the Adirondacks southwest of Saratoga Springs, Johnston's is the most northerly of the Hudson Valley wineries. This site is of little concern to winemaker Kurt Johnston, as he specializes in apple wine and honey wine, or mead.

Johnston's first release, McIntosh Apple Wine, is made entirely from McIntosh apples grown near Altamont 30 or 40 miles south. Johnston sweetens the juice before fermenting it to bring its alcohol up to about 12%. The resulting wine exhibits clean apple flavor and has good balance. He plans to add a selection of apple wines made from the Cortland, Northern Spy, and Macoun varieties.

Johnston also produces an apple and honey wine, McIntosh Mead, which has lively fruit and honey character, as well as a traditional mead and a 100% blueberry wine, vinified dry. His blueberry wine has many of the aroma and flavor attributes of Cabernet Sauvignon or Merlot, and even has their rich purple color. "In a recent blind tasting," Johnston adds, "some pretty experienced people thought it was a Napa Valley Cabernet. I get a kick out of that."

5140 Bliss Road, Ballston Spa, NY 12020; 518 882-6310. Closed Mondays. The winery is on Bliss Road, 3 miles east of Galway Village.

East of the River

No poem was ever written by
a drinker of water.

HORACE
65-8 BC
Roman Poet

North Salem Vineyard

ESTABLISHED 1964

NORTH SALEM

North Salem, of all Hudson Valley wineries, is closest to Manhattan. Founded by Dr. George Naumburg, a practicing New York City physician, the site's proximity to the city was a key reason for its selection. In addition, Naumburg explains, "I thought the area showed great promise for wine grape production. And it was the place of my childhood."

In 1964, Naumburg and his wife, Michelle, purchased the dairy farm that occupied this site and immediately set to work finding the most suitable wine grapes. "At first, we planted 36 different varieties, experimenting to determine which thrive in this location." Of those, four were selected as consistent producers of superior wine: the white varietal Seyval Blanc and the reds Foch, DeChaunac, and

Chancellor. Today, the vineyard comprises 18 acres, most planted in Seyval Blanc.

The winery occupies a barn, built in 1947, with a dramatic vaulted ceiling. From the tasting room, visitors may walk to a deck overlooking the vineyard.

North Salem produces five wines: a reserve white that is mostly Seyval Blanc with some Ravat and Vidal; a reserve red that blends Foch, DeChaunac, and Chancellor; a rosé produced by a tincture of red wine added to Seyval; a sweet red; and a Seyval-based sparkling wine made in the classic méthode champenoise.

North Salem wines are not oak-aged, but instead produced in stainless steel vessels. This process, Naumburg maintains, "assures a clean product and preserves the integrity of the fruit's natural character."

R.R. 2, Hardscrabble & Delancey Roads, North Salem, NY 10560; 914-669-5518. Open daily, May to November. Open weekends all year. Travel north on Route 684 to exit 8, turn right on Hardscrabble Road and travel 2½ miles.

Amberleaf Vineyards

ESTABLISHED 1987

WAPPINGERS FALLS

Not far from the picturesque river hamlet of Chelsea sits Amberleaf Vineyards. Although co-owner and wine-maker Ronald Plimley grows twelve grape varieties, the usual output of 1,000 gallons makes Amberleaf one of New York's smallest wineries.

Plimley's interest in wine began in 1960 soon after his marriage to Theresa, his Italian-American wife. "We would frequently visit her family," he relates, "where we shared wine as part of the mealtime tradition. This was a new experience for me."

In 1974, Plimley bought some grapes and made his own wine. As he gained experience, fascination turned to passion. In 1979, the Plimleys purchased their current property and planted their first grapes, all European vinifera, in 1982.

Plimley has opted to keep the operation small, striving to make a variety of quality wines. He has since learned that being small has two sides. "On the one hand," he explains, "the Culinary Institute liked our Chardonnay enough to buy virtually my entire supply. On the other, I had little left to share with friends and customers."

Amberleaf wines are made from the European varieties Chardonnay, Riesling, Cabernet Franc, Merlot, and Carmine; as well as the hybrids Seyval,

Vidal, and Chambourcin. Blends represent the majority of the production. Amberleaf's biggest seller is Une Tranche de Vie (a slice of life), made from Vidal, Seyval Blanc, and Riesling. Wappingers Red is a blend of red grapes and Petite Arm Noir is a sweet wine made from seedless grapes. All Amberleaf wines are estate-bottled and many spend time in American oak.

River Road North, Wappingers Falls, NY 12590; 914-831-4362. Open daily. Follow Route 84 to exit 11 and travel north for 3¾ miles on 9D. Turn left on Old State Road, then left on River Road North.

Millbrook Vineyards

ESTABLISHED 1981

MILLBROOK

Visitors to Millbrook approach the winery's buildings by a meandering drive through the vineyards' meticulously cultivated slopes. Each vine, each row, each section, is carefully placed and dressed. You immediately sense that this is an establishment committed to producing fine wine.

As the winery's large Dutch hip-roofed barn comes into view, the scope that owner John S. Dyson envisioned for the enterprise also becomes apparent. Millbrook has approximately 60 acres of grape vines, all classic European varieties. Almost half are Chardonnay and a third are Pinot Noir, reflecting Dyson's belief that this part of the Hudson Valley is suitable for making Burgundian-style wines. The classic red grapes of Bordeaux are also present, with 10 acres planted in Cabernet Sauvignon, Merlot, and Cabernet Franc.

Millbrook grows and experiments with more European grape varieties than any winery in New York and thus functions as something of a viticultural research station. (This may not be surprising given Dyson's former role as New York State Commissioner of Agriculture). All told, there are some 25 varieties at Millbrook, including the Italian Nebbiolo, Sangiovese, and Tocai Friulano; the French Gamay Noir, and the Alsatian Gewürztraminer.

Millbrook produced its first commercial vintage in 1985. Along with Dyson, general manager David Bova and winemaker John Graziano contribute their talents to the operation. The winery has state-of-the-art equipment and classic French cooperage. The entrance and sales and tasting rooms overlook the vineyard which occupies a long slope facing south and west above a dramatic Hudson Valley landscape.

Millbrook presently offers Chardonnay, Pinot Noir, a méthode champenoise sparkling wine made from these grapes, Cabernet Sauvignon, Cabernet Franc, and Hunt Country Red, a flavorsome blend of several reds.

R.R. 1, Box 167D, Wing & Shunpike Roads, Millbrook, NY 12545; 914-677-8383. Open daily. From Taconic Parkway, take 44 east to 82 north. Travel 3½ miles to Shunpike Road, then turn right and drive 3 miles to winery.

Clinton Vineyards

ESTABLISHED 1975

CLINTON CORNERS

The Seyval Blanc grape and Clinton Vineyards have had a long and successful marriage. Founder and winemaker Ben Feder uses this delicious and versatile grape in virtually all his wines.

Feder was a graphic designer from New York City who came to this bucolic setting in Dutchess County known for its purebred horse and cattle breeding. After several years of raising Black Angus cows and steers, Feder became fascinated with the Hudson Valley's rich viticultural history and decided to grow grapes and make wine himself. "I soon realized I was better suited to caring for grapevines than looking after steers," he recalls. "I was also challenged by the prospect of producing the best Hudson Valley wine possible."

Feder began by planting four acres of Seyval Blanc on these hills previously used as pasture. His research convinced him that Seyval was the ideal grape for this region. By 1976, Feder's acreage had more than doubled. When his first vintage was released in 1977, *The New York Times* called it "one of the best wines produced in the East."

In addition to his flagship Seyval Blanc, Feder produces Seyval Naturel, a sparkling wine with Champagne-like toastiness and creamy texture. When the summer growing season is relatively warm and dry, Feder produces a Riesling from the one acre of vines he tends. 1991 was such a summer and Feder released a limited number of half-bottles of this luscious dessert wine done in the German Auslese style.

The winery occupies one of the property's two 19th-century dairy barns. Feder added an extension to the barn for producing his sparkling wines in the méthode champenoise. "The real advantage to being located

in this cool micro-climate," says Feder, "is that when disgorging time comes, all we have to do is open the doors and Mother Nature does the chilling."

Schultzville Road, Clinton Corners, NY 12514; 914-266-5372. Open weekends and holidays. The winery is just off Schultzville Road, north of Clinton Corners and slightly west of the Taconic Parkway.

Cascade Mountain Winery

ESTABLISHED 1972

AMENIA

William Wetmore, owner of Cascade Mountain, is a novelist who moved from New York City to these rolling hills to find solitude in which to write. "I found I missed the wines I had become accustomed to in New York," he explains, "so I just decided to make my own. Since I favor red wines, the first vines I planted bore red grapes." While Wetmore still maintains his emphasis on reds, he produces a significant amount of white wine from grapes he buys from local vineyards.

The winery's Private Reserve Red is made from Cabernet Sauvignon with some Leon Millot and has pleasing berry aromas and flavors. The Dry Red Wine blends the hybrids Leon Millot and Baco Noir. Among whites, Cascade produces a Seyval Blanc and a Private Reserve White, the latter a blend of Chardonnay and Seyval Blanc that was selected as the official reception wine for the United States Mission to the United Nations.

Cascade Mountain is known for the humorous proprietary names on some of its labels. At one time, the winery introduced Le Hamburgér Red, Pardonnez-Moi, and Spring Fever. Current labels include Summertide, a fruity picnic white; Harvest Rosé made from the Chancellor grape; Villager, a soft fruity red; and two dessert wines—Heavenly Dazes and a rich, late-harvest Vignoles.

Visitors to the winery are invited to take a self-guided tour which con-

cludes in an upstairs tasting room and gift shop. One of Cascade Mountain's attractions is its well-regarded restaurant. The luncheon menu features regional specialties: goat's milk cheese, smoked trout, salmon mousse, duck patés, locally raised fowl, and vegetables in season. Dinner is a more for-

mal affair and features several courses with matching wines.

Flint Hill Road, Amenia, NY 12501; 914-373-9021. Open daily; reservations for restaurant. Travel 3 miles north of Amenia on Route 22, then left on Webatuck School Road and follow signs to winery.

The Meadery at Greenwich

ESTABLISHED 1989

GREENWICH

Considering the wide range of wines and other agricultural products from the Hudson Valley, it is not surprising to find a meadery. Mead, considered the "Vikings' wine of inspiration," is made from fermented honey and water. The Meadery at Greenwich is the joint venture of Robert and Margaret Stevens, successful beekeepers, and Wayne Thygesen, one of their best customers and an accomplished mead maker.

The Meadery produces a variety of wines with names and labels inspired by Viking mythology and folklore. Odin's Traditional Mead, for example, is produced by the ancient firebrewed method, in which honey and water are boiled together, then oakaged for at least two years. This mead

has a distinctive, slightly sweet and malted character. Odin's Dry mead, a considerably lighter and drier wine, is produced with modern filtering methods.

The Meadery produces three other wines. Idun's Apple Mead is a flavor-

ful wine made from apple cider and honey, a blend known as a cyser. Thor's Raspberry Mead, produced from local hand-picked raspberries and clover honey, is a mellow, succulent dessert wine. (A berry-flavored mead is called a malomel.) And Loki's Spiced Mead is a fragrant wine meant to be served warm.

Even at the Meadery's relatively remote location in the northeastern reaches of the Hudson Valley, sales are brisk. Total production in 1991 was 15,000 gallons and the 1991 Traditional Mead was sold out early in 1992.

Route 29 at Meader Road, Greenwich, NY 12834; 518-692-9669. Closed Sundays. The winery is on Meader Road, north of Greenwich.

Glossary

Grape Varieties of the Hudson River Valley

Tradition, soil, climate, and man's pioneering spirit have combined to bless the Hudson River Valley with a diverse array of grape varieties. The following is a summary of those grown in the valley and used in commercially produced wines.

For clarity, varieties have been placed in three categories: Hybrid, European, and American. It should be noted, however, that most European varieties reflect hybridization over thousands of years, while most American varieties result from some 200 years of hybridization. Here, "Hybrid" refers to French-American crosses that have much of the elegant flavor of a European varietal and the hardiness characteristic of American grapes.

Note: (w) indicates a white-wine grape; (r) indicates a red-wine grape. A pink wine, or rosé, is made by reducing skin contact during the processing of a red-wine grape or by adding a small amount of red wine to a white wine.

HYBRID VARIETIES

AURORE (w) A mildly fruity, fragrant wine grape sometimes used alone but often blended. It produces dry, semi-sweet, and dessert wines.

BACO NOIR (r) A grape which produces medium to full-bodied wines with firm acid. When young, the wine can have a strong, grassy character and benefits from oak and bottle aging. It is often used as a blending wine or to tint rosé wines.

CAYUGA (w) A grape developed at Geneva, New York, which produces delicate, fruity wine. It can be made dry to semi-sweet.

CHAMBOURCIN (r) Its rich, spicy fruit flavor lends itself to a variety of styles, from full-bodied to light. It possesses good acid and, when aged in oak, is often hard to distinguish from a classic European variety.

CHANCELLOR (r) A grape capable of producing rich, full-bodied, complex wines, especially when aged in oak.

CHELOIS (r) This grape is usually used to make a medium-bodied, fruity varietal for blending or to produce a rosé.

DeCHAUNAC (r) A grape that can make a dark wine with a distinct grassy flavor. Typically crisp and tart, DeChaunac produces a medium-bodied red when aged in oak. It can also produce a dry, fruity rosé.

FOCH (r) Possessing herbaceous qualities and firm acid, this grape is well-suited to making nouveau-style wine, a flavorful rosé, or a full-bodied red. Its ancestry includes Pinot Noir.

HORIZON (w) Similar to Cayuga and Aurore in producing fruity wines, this grape flourishes in the cooler northern Hudson Valley climate.

LANDOT NOIR (r) A grape that makes fruity, crisp, full-bodied wines with good tannins. It can also produce a spicy, fruity nouveau and rosé.

LEON MILLOT (r) Often mistaken for a European variety, this is a versatile grape with rich fruit and firm tannins that makes full-bodied reds, nouveau-style wines, or flavorful rosés.

RAVAT 51 OR VIGNOLES (w) A grape with distinctive aroma and fruitiness that is superior as a dry wine, but has sufficient acid to produce a well-balanced dessert wine, especially when harvested late. Its parentage includes Chardonnay.

RAYON D'OR (w) A grape that produces austere, often spicy, and aromatic wines with good acid struc-ture. While usually found in blends, it is appealing when used alone.

SEYVAL BLANC (w) Often called the Queen of White Hybrids, this grape produces clean, fresh wine with delicious and often wide-ranging fruit aromas and flavors. Seyval Blanc usually makes fruity off-dry wines, but can also produce fine oak-aged dry wine as well as superior sparkling.

VERDELET (w) A grape producing wine of tart, flinty character. It is usually a component of dry sparkling wine to enhance acid structure.

VIDAL (w) A grape that produces fresh, crisp wine with spicy, floral characteristics and melon or pineapple-like fruitiness, similar to a Riesling. Because it has good acid, it is versatile and makes a honeyed late-harvest dessert wine.

EUROPEAN VARIETIES

CABERNET FRANC (r) Although used in France primarily as part of a blend, the grape by itself makes spicy, complex, medium-bodied dry wine.

CABERNET SAUVIGNON (r) The classic red grape of Bordeaux and California. When aged in oak, it produces rich, complex, and aromatic wines that soften with age. Vineyard yields tend to be low and demand high, resulting in premium prices.

CHARDONNAY (w) The classic white grape of France's Burgundy region and the leading white-wine grape in America, Chardonnay produces wine styles ranging from light and fruity to rich, buttery, and complex. Low yields and high demand usually push prices toward the upper end.

CARMINE (r) A cross of several European varieties, this grape produces rich and complex wine.

GAMAY (GAMAY NOIR) (r) This classic grape of the Beaujolais region of France produces fruity cherry and often peppery wine, usually done in a light to medium-bodied style.

GEWÜRZTRAMINER (w) The soul of the Alsace region of France, this grape produces a spicy wine with fruity overtones.

MERLOT (r) A classic grape from Bordeaux that also flourishes in America, Merlot is often used in blends to soften Cabernet Sauvignon. The wine by itself is supple, yet rich and fruity and often complex.

MUSCAT (w) A wide range of grapes with a distinctive spicy herbal character. It is delightful sweet or dry.

Pinot Noir (r) The noble red grape of Burgundy and Oregon, Pinot Noir can yield wine with complex herbal, earthy and cherry aromas and flavors. When not pressed on the skins, it can also produce juice for sparkling wine (as in Champagne). It is often difficult to grow, resulting in high prices.

Riesling (w) The heart of the great white wines of Germany, this grape imparts a wide range of fruity and aromatic qualities and can also have spicy, floral characteristics. When harvested late, it can make exquisite dessert wine.

American Varieties

Catawba (w) The grape makes a delightful sparkling wine that won first-place medals in Europe during the mid-19th century. Its wine is fruity, fragrant, and moderately grapey with firm acid.

Concord (r) An American cross developed in Massachusetts and one of America's most common table grapes, Concord produces wine of deep color and a tangy grapey aroma and taste. Although usually made sweet, Concord also makes an interesting off-dry wine.

Delaware (w) The grape makes attractive floral wines, in both semi-sweet and sweet styles.

Dutchess (w) Developed in the Hudson River Valley, this grape produces wine with attractive fruit and floral characteristics. One of the few wines made from native American grapes that will improve with time in oak cooperage and the bottle.

Niagara (w) This grape produces wine of intense grapey flavor, usually balanced by the addition of sugar.

Steuben (r) Developed at the Geneva Research Station in the Finger Lakes, Steuben produces a fruity, spicy, muscat-like wine.

~~~~~ *Bibliography* ~~~~~

Aaron, Jan. *Wine Routes of America*. New York: Dutton, 1989.

Adams, Leon D. *The Wines of America*, 4th Ed. New York: McGraw-Hill, 1990.

Boyle, Robert H. *The Hudson River: A Natural and Unnatural History*. New York: Norton, 1969.

Cattell, Hudson, and Lee Stauffer Miller. *Wine East of the Rockies*. Lancaster, PA: L & H Photojournalism, 1982.

Crosby, Everett. *The Vintage Years: The Story of High Tor Vineyards*. New York: Harper & Row, 1973.

Dial, Tom. *The Wines of New York*. Utica, NY: North Country Books, 1986.

Ensrud, Barbara. *American Vineyards*. New York: Stewart, Tabori & Chang, 1988.

Establishment of the Hudson River Region Viticultural Area. BATF: Federal Register. Vol. 47. No. 108. June 4, 1982.

Fadiman, Clifton, and Sam Aaron. *The Joys of Wine*. Ed. Darlene Geis. New York: Abrams, 1975.

Fosdick, Lucian John. *The French Blood in America*. Baltimore: Genealogical Publishing Company; reprint of 1906 edition.

Fulling, Edmund H. "Yew Trees and Vineyards of Croton Point." *The Garden Journal* (July-August 1960), pp. 125-37.

Hedrick, U.P., assisted by N.O. Booth, O.M. Taylor, R. Wellington, N.J. Dorsey. *The Grapes of New York: 15th Annual Report*. Vol. 3. Part II (State of New York: Department of Agriculture), 1908.

Keller, Allan. *Life Along the Hudson*. Tarrytown, New York: Sleepy Hollow Restorations, 1976.

Lichine, Alexis. *New Encyclopedia of Wines & Spirits*. 3rd Ed. New York: Knopf, 1981.

Miller, Mark. *Wine: A Gentleman's Game*. New York: Harper & Row, 1984.

Morton, Lucie T. *Winegrowing in Eastern America*. Ithaca: Cornell University Press, 1985.

Mulligan, Tim. *The Hudson River Valley*. New York: Random House, 1985.

New York Wine Course and Reference. Penn Yan, New York: New York Wine & Grape Foundation, n.d.

O'Brien, Raymond J. *American Sublime: Landscape and Scenery of the Lower Hudson Valley*. New York: Columbia University Press, 1981.

Pinney, Thomas. *A History of Wine in America*. Berkeley: University of California Press, 1989.

Vine, Richard P. *Wine Appreciation*. New York: Facts on File, 1988.

Acknowledgments

For early and unwavering support of this book:
Martha Borgeson, Barbara Ensrud, William Moffett, Peter Morrell,
Burton Notarius, James Tresize, Michael Turback, and Kevin Zraly

For making us feel at home during our journeys through the Valley:
Michelle Dreeman

For providing a wealth of little-known information on the Valley's history:
Christopher Letts

For creating photographs capturing the beauty of the Valley
and the character of its wineries: Laury Egan

For editing our manuscript with toughness and rigor while
honoring the spirit of our message: Carolyn Maxwell

For conceiving and directing this project with steady enthusiasm:
John Tucker

And especially, for their support, patience and devotion:
our wives Karen and Dorothy

ALAN R. MARTELL
ALTON LONG